CLASSIC GARDENS · ERICA LENNARD

WITH AN INTRODUCTION BY WILLIAM HOWARD ADAMS

LUSTRUM PRESS

ALL RIGHTS RESERVED UNDER INTERNATIONAL
AND PAN-AMERICAN COPYRIGHT CONVENTIONS.
PUBLISHED IN THE UNITED STATES OF AMERICA
BY LUSTRUM PRESS, INC., BOX 450
CANAL STREET STATION, NEW YORK, N.Y. 10013

COPYRIGHT © 1982, LUSTRUM PRESS, INC.

JOHN FLATTAU, RALPH GIBSON AND ARNE LEWIS
PRODUCED BY JOHN FLATTAU
EDITED BY RALPH GIBSON
DESIGNED BY ARNE LEWIS

MANUFACTURED IN THE UNITED STATES OF AMERICA
LIBRARY OF CONGRESS CATALOGUE CARD #83-80908
ISBN: 0-912810-38-6 (HARDCOVER)

POUR ALEXANDRE QUI M'A FAIT DÉCOUVRIR LES JARDINS.

CAN YOU DIG IT?

The garden—especially the monumental European creations of the 17th and 18th centuries—has defied all but the most talented artists to record adequately. The extensive scale of the massive, sprawling baroque gardens such as Versailles, inspired a whole school of "birds eye" view artists who attempted to project in drawing and print a coherent picture of the spectacular layout from an imaginary point of view a few hundred feet above the ground.

Gardens are still hard to document even with a camera and in many ways are akin to architecture and the dance as notoriously difficult photographic subjects. Each art form seems to generate its own set of problems for the camera, problems that are only rarely surmounted. Nothing in the stiff photographs of Nijinsky, for example, matches the contemporary description of those who actually saw him and were so moved by his magic, vital presence on the stage. In photographs of architecture, the enlargement of some detail of design, or destruction of scale by a dramatic aiming of the camera lens can distort the subject beyond any relationship to the actual structure. The constantly changing quality of gardens creates a further photographic difficulty that often leaves the viewer with an unsatisfied feeling because of this dimension of time which photographs cannot deal with.

No matter how often we have visited the park at Versailles or Stowe or the garden of the Villa Lante, our experience is always different in spite of the familiar landmarks and topography. For our emotions, obsessions and physical responses have changed and are forever changing just as the garden is constantly transformed. The rich, sensual textures of nature unite and then dissolve among the formal elements of stone, water, sculpture, and architecture, while our own continuously changing place in the composition makes it one of our most moving experiences. Yet the memory of a garden, like the memory of a former lover can fade quickly. The residue of a few hardly recognizable photographs only heightens one's sense of loss at the passing of an affair that had once seemed so fixed and lasting.

But if one has had the pleasure of knowing the actual gardens that Erica Lennard has documented in this collection, there can be no room for disappointment in her souvenirs. The images selected, the right degree of light sensitively employed for a particular site; the abstract, formal elements that have a special appeal for her eye present the contemporary viewer with discrete, self-contained creations, that are outside the reach of and discontinuous with the mere history of each place. There is a sensitivity that concentrates in the camera's perspective and composition that somehow penetrates the esthetic intentions of the historic creators of a particular garden—even though definitive artistic signatures on early garden designs are almost as rare as on a petroglyph at Chaco Canyon or the artificial mound at Silbury Hill in Wiltshire, England.

While I have had the advantage of knowing—with whatever certainty one can ever *know* a garden—each of the gardens that Lennard has recorded, I am touched with the same feeling that Roland Barthes describes in his essay on photography CAMERA LUCIDA as he studied a 19th century photograph of the Alhambra. "Looking at these landscapes of predilection, it is as if *I were certain* of having been there" entering the scene in a specific, palpable way at the moment the photograph was made.

What is the source of this almost physical attraction of being drawn out of time into one of Lennard's gardens in Italy, France, or England? Is it the way that the light defines the stone coping on the edge of the grand canal at Versailles (Page 15). The arcadian, English mist that frames Vantbrugh's bridge at Blenheim Palace (Page 105). The joining of the great stairs, *le grand degrée* at Chantilly (Page 47). When I contemplate one of Lennard's prints I can easily believe myself to be there within the picture, possessed by the beauty of the magic combination of architecture with light, water, trees, and earth. Even though Lennard has chosen some of the most extravagantly dream-like garden settings imaginable, one does not at all feel a victim in mere fantasy or hallucination.

The quality of *place* which Lennard manages to convey also enables me to identify each particular garden fragment by some hidden signature of *locus* which the photograph has isolated even without detailed labels or captions. This is all the more remarkable when one considers the mythical quality with which she invests her subject by simply concentrating on the essentials in the most straightforward way. It is a pictorial strategy that echoes that of Eugene Atget, notably in her compositions of "empty stages," though Lennard is by no means a mere follower of that great garden photographer. Given the ephemeral quality of earth, trees, plants, and water, her's and Atget's images are all the more astonishing in their psychological "intentions," fixing for us with the barest of props and stage furniture, a kind of theatrical essence, a stage set that manages to convey the imprint of an entire society or culture. Great stage designers possess the same genius.

The idea of the garden as theater, if not new in early Renaissance Europe, certainly picks up momentum in the more sophisticated, noble Italian gardens of the 16th century in their extravagant, theatrical settings which glorified a particular relationship between men and nature. The theater of staged fêtes, masques and pageants— involving hordes of actors, *corps de ballet*, extravagant costumes, music and on occasion wild animals—were an integral part of idealized aristocratic court life. The scale of such presentations and the physical dimensions of the court gardens grew and developed as outdoor spaces for dramatic productions in response to the widespread use of royal gardens as the setting for these spectacular political gestures.

In France the pageantry of the royal entry of the 16th century which was originally staged in city streets was gradually transformed and adapted to fit the king's gardens at Fountainebleau, the Tuileries, and ultimately Versailles. The elements of stagecraft and statecraft were merged to express royal power within the open-air environment of the palace gardens where choreography, drama, and music were used to define and to celebrate the social and political order.

We see the horizontal line of the apron of the stage actually becoming a factor in French garden design of the 17th century, the backdrop often composed of real palaces or temples of stone framed with real trees to create an enormously versatile performing area where illusion and reality were deliberately confused. Some of the extraordinary horizontal planes and spatial compositions that dominate the composition of the French classical garden grow out of this theatrical function which has been all but lost in the 20th century "theme park" which many of the former royal gardens have become.

In the gardens of Vaux, Versailles, St. Cloud, and Sceaux, one frequently comes to a cross-axis, a terrace or fountain basin and discovers a perfect stage or playing area that need only the actors and courtiers to animate it. Often an imaginary proscenium arch is suggested by towering trees, or the apron line of the stage is established by the simple placement of two ancient urns at what becomes the two corners of the playing area. Walking through a succession of bare "stages" in 17th and 18th century gardens one often feels the same feeling of melancholy one experiences on entering an empty theater or auditorium without the animation of actors, sets, lighting, audience to produce the buzz of dramatic expectation. There is, for example an engraving by Silvestre of a court ballet staged in the *Tapis Vert* with the real palace of Versailles serving as the illusory background that corresponds closely to Lennard's photograph of the same scene (Page 11).

It is interesting to note not only the number of horizontal framings within the present collection of photographs but also the use of theatrical compositions, compositions that seem so fitting for the subject. The precise focus and depth of field of the allée at the Parc de Sceaux (Page 41) could be easily translated into a projected ballet stage-set with no alterations. For a change of scene, one could turn with equal finesse to a setting from Marly (Pages 31 and 35) Saint Cloud (Page 69) or Chantilly (Page 49).

Just as framing and perspective has been a part of painting since the early Renaissance, the same framing and Albertian perspective also functions in photography and by extension is very much a part of the stage. When we consider the important role that the theater has played in the evolution of the European garden, it is not surprising that the theatrical aspects of the garden should be conveyed to us through the intermediary of the camera.

Unlike the garden itself—the moving, existential encounter with nature that is civilized beyond our ability to take it in completely and with any "certainty,"—the image of the photograph can be looked at and studied to whatever degree of "intensity" (Barthes' word) we choose. It is this ability and willingness to concentrate our glances on Lennard's tableaux, summoning up out of their mystery whatever evidence our perceptions and reveries are capable of.

The first photograph that I saw of Erica Lennard's work was that of Marly (Page 33) Louis XIV's retreat looking down the main avenue from the height of the old entrance where the king passed with increasing frequency in the last two decades of his life in his attempt to escape his prison at Versailles. There at the bottom of what had once been a narrow, unpromising "sewer of a valley into which the surrounding countryside drained itself," as the Duc de Saint Simone describes it we can see the outlines of all that is left of the king's weekend palace marked out by stone foundations. To the 20th century eye, the abstract image is perhaps closer to contemporary artists like Robert Smithson or Margaret Hicks than the obliterated world of the Sun King. Stripped of its pavilions and courtesans, we, like Barthes, see only a photograph "without signification yet summoning up the depth of any possible meaning, unrevealed yet manifest, having that absence-as presence which constitutes the lure and the fascination of the Sirens."

Each of Lennard's garden photographs, intimate fragments of a public art, can best be read in private meditation. This is perhaps the only way to reconcile the *public and the private* by contemplating "the thereness of the past and the lost reality which rules out nostalgia" as Clive James recently remarked. In confronting the reality of the historic garden as a damaged but surviving artifact—once a model for what the world hoped to become—Lennard has understood the limits that reality imposes on the photographer, In accepting those limitations with brilliance and humility, she reiterates the irretrievable vision that must have defined and guided the original creation of the gardens themselves.

WILLIAM HOWARD ADAMS

RAMBOUILLET

VERSAILLES

VERSAILLES

VERSAILLES

VERSAILLES

VERSAILLES

VERSAILLES

VERSAILLES

VERSAILLES, POTAGER DE ROI

VERSAILLES, POTAGER DE ROI

VERSAILLES, PETIT TRIANON

MARLY-LE-ROI

MARLY-LE-ROI

MARLY-LE-ROI

MARLY-LE-ROI

PARC DE SCEAUX

PARC DE SCEAUX

PARC DE SCEAUX

PARC DE SCEAUX

TUILERIES

CHANTILLY

CHANTILLY

CHATEAU DE BRECY

VILLANDRY

COMPEÌGNE

COMPEÌGNE

CHATEAU DE RARAY

COURANCES

GIVERNY

GIVERNY

CHATEAU DE MONTGEOFFROY

PARC DE ST. CLOUD

PARC DE ST. CLOUD

PARC DE ST. CLOUD

VILLA D'ESTE

VILLA D'ESTE

VILLA D'ESTE

VILLA D'ESTE

VILLA D'ESTE

VILLA D'ESTE

VILLA LANTE

VILLA LANTE

VILLA LANTE

VILLA LANTE

VILLA VALMARANA DEI NANI

BOMARZO

VILLA ROTUNDA

GIARDINI GIUSTI

GIARDINI GIUSTI

BLENHEIM

BLENHEIM

BLENHEIM

BLENHEIM

SISSINGHURST

ROUSHAM

CLIVEDEN

CLIVEDEN

OXFORD BOTANICAL GARDEN

HEVER CASTLE

HUSH HEATH

PARC DE SCEAUX, SELF-PORTRAIT

★

DATE DUE			